Sinbad the Sailor

Illustrated by Val Biro

Award Publications Limited

There once lived a man called Sinbad. He was rich and generous, but it was a mystery how his riches had come about.

One evening Sinbad ordered his servant to invite a man begging outside his house to join him for dinner.

"Tonight I will tell you the story of my riches. As a reward for listening I shall give you a bag of gold," said Sinbad.

When I was young, began Sinbad, I sailed far across the oceans, buying and selling goods.
On one voyage our ship found a small island. We rowed over to it and lit a fire to cook.

When we lit the fire, the island began to shake and tremble. It was not an island at all but a great sea monster!

My friends fled in the boat, but I was thrown into the sea.

I clung to a piece of wood and floated in the sea for many days. Eventually, I found land.

A soldier found me and took me to see his king.

The king was very kind and gave me food and shelter in his palace by the harbour.

One day, a ship sailed into the harbour.

It was my old ship!
And all my things were still there.

I sold my cargo for lots of money then sailed home.

On my next voyage, our ship stopped at a large island. I took a nap while the other sailors explored.

When I awoke, I was alone. I searched for the crew, but found only an enormous egg.

Suddenly, a huge bird swooped down and carried me off.

It dropped me into a valley filled with diamonds and giant snakes. There was no way out!

As the snakes fell asleep in the sun, some men arrived. They threw meat down and it stuck to the diamonds. Then huge eagles carried the meat back up to the men.

This gave me an idea. I filled my bag with diamonds and tied a piece of meat to my back. Just as I had hoped, an eagle carried me out of the valley.

The men saw me and shouted so the eagle dropped me. I landed with a bump – and a fortune in jewels in my bag!

As I walked back to find the ship, I saw that the crew had found the giant egg and cooked it. This made me sad, so I left them to their meal.

The enormous birds saw that their egg had been eaten and chased the crew. As they tried to sail away, the birds dropped stones on the ship and sank it.

Once again I was stranded. But I was lucky, and soon another boat arrived.

The crew invited me to join them on a coconut hunt.

We didn't even need to climb to get them. We threw stones up into the trees and monkeys hurled coconuts back at us!

As we sailed home, we sold the coconuts at markets along the way for a very good price.

"I have been very lucky and met many kind people," smiled Sinbad, "so now I share my wealth with people in need."